Daughter of Wednesday

by Abbie Amy

Illustrated by Marta Alvim
House of Illustrology

DAUGHTER OF WEDNESDAY
COPYRIGHT © 2020 ABBIE AMY

ALL RIGHTS RESERVED. No part of this publication may be reproduced, stored or transmitted in any form written, or electronic without prior permission from the author, except in the case of brief quotation embodied in critical reviews and certain other non-commercial uses as permitted by copyright law.

Cover Design by Andrew Fraser

ISBN 978-1-9160492-3-9

*To Andrew, for the times you carried my
heart when I found it too heavy.*

The Epilogue at the Beginning

He will recognise these words
for I gave them to him first
And the water is but a body of salt
it's of my old skin
of my old hope
I no longer hold the promise
of a single light bulb
and that is the release
the real tide making its way back to me
But reflection is in the water
in my iris I still see us
holding hands and letting the credits roll
Now you are titled with new love
me with acceptance
with relief that I am allowed to keep doors open
so that I can walk through them

Hope greets me on the other side
she says
*That was beautiful
and now we wait for him too?*
I shake my head

*We no longer wait
for those who could so easily
cast me aside*

and she smiles

*Daughter of Wednesday
you have arrived*

One

Wednesday

He says
on the last night of July
I saw the future
when I looked into your eyes
I hold my breath
I'll wait for the reprise
I'm always going to
with every atom in me
Could you love me again and again?
The way the sun and moon fall
only to rise
I'm always going—
We fall asleep the way
we did the first night
When we wake
it's no longer July

London

Someone emptied all the milk cartons
They're on the counter
little apartment statues
The alarm doesn't go off
The light switches don't turn on
The refrigerator has lost its hum
The kitchen is empty
much like this city
How were we in the beginning?
I swear a past life warned me
that love means
the grave is coming

Where are you?
What did we do?

Why do I have the feeling
that I have always known you?

Of Love, of Light

We fell in love
then watched as the news flashed before us
our mouths little circles
The city of love
The city of light
vandalised
The people of love, of light
criminalised
So we turned from the screen
but realised
that we were living in the scene
The ends of my hair were on fire
My friend took out her scissors and cut it shorter
They won't even notice the difference

It's all his fault! she cried
and I just cried
The tears don't wash the stains away
but eventually they'll dry

I found her moving her clothes into my room
*I need to stitch myself in
so they can't make me move!*
It appeared logical to help
but perhaps I should have used
threads of steel
so the fates could not have unravelled
the plans we had mapped out

It's all his fault! my fractured self cried out
and together we cried
The tears don't wash the stains away
there's nowhere love can't hide

She climbed up on the window sill
the night blinking back at her
the moon was not yet full

I'll do it!
she promised
You know that I will!

Only if you take me with you

She trembled
her upper lip no longer still
You're meant to plead with me
No, my love
I have accepted that
people always leave

Of love, of light
we were two friends
two fraternal candles
loving
wax dripping
we burnt out in plain sight

Still
I laid down all my matches
I let them spell out hope
She peered at them and pulled me in
Her embrace felt like acceptance

We sat on the window sill in silence
Perhaps love had no intention to end
The city was on fire
but maybe there was wicker
still left inside a friend

The First Week

My skin weeps
The hair atop my head
falls three times asleep
I wade into hot water
Each effort
coming up shorter
I am the daughter
I am without
We were just a second
A mourning of sound

I remember the smell of his room
The grey and white jumper
The hands over my ears
Mine over his chest
his throbbing heart
Am I the first?
It doesn't matter
I promise you I'm fine
Basements
Bridges
Arguments
I remember it all the time

The Bar on Long Acre

If I move on a Tuesday
will you come over the following day?
The air is polluted with loneliness
I see it on their faces
in this place we're incarcerated
The walls are wet with paint
they rolled out new carpet just for me
but I still keep my shelf in the fridge
empty

It's a sin to go where my footprints stand
cemented in the pavement
my exit played out by the jazz band
I mark a map with little red crosses
go by on foot and ignore the losses
The bar on Long Acre beckons me in
stretching her arms around my back
She snaps my spine
as if I'm a second-hand paperback

It's the realisation of everything I despise
dancing on top of me
Everyone in this bar
is everyone in this city
Vacant eyes but hearts that scream
I'm not alone but I'm lonely
why don't you take five minutes
to try to get to know me

My train is coming
hear it turning
On Wednesday morning
I wait for the knock on my door
I wait and wait
like the audience
hungry for the encore

Daisy

She came into the world
on a Friday at two-thirty
a beautiful afternoon baby
a glowing winter daisy
Her mother cried as she gave life
and I cried for life
For the anticipated days
the agony
the pain
that this little flower
who didn't ask to be born
will have to encounter
The loss
the leaving
the understanding
that most love is fleeting
I cried for life
I cried for the petals falling
I cried for what was coming

Indefinite

I am indefinite
bound by miscommunication
and the realisation
that my edges are softer
than first perception

He took my grandmother's watch
broke it
gold flakes rubbing off
like time passing through us
I wasn't awake enough apparently
It was him
that boy stole the hours from me
He called me at school
to take away in words
what I had laid out on a hanger
I thought we were dressing for tomorrow
Did I fight out of love or just anger?

We are indefinite

That was
and wasn't
the end

At least that's what I tell myself
I'm simply playing pretend

Get Over It

It's like staring into a spotlight
a headlight
a surgical light
any kind of obnoxious light you like
Of course there are tears in my eyes
You try looking at the sun
and being the one not to cry
I walk every street naked
Some people laugh
some people deal in sympathy
some people are so over the lack of dignity
But I live in memory
and it scratches my flesh
my chest
my breast
The heaviness I inhale is posing as air
Hurt snags like branches with no leaves
(they used to mean possibility)
Blood blossoms
I wipe it clean
It seeps deeper in
Everywhere I go is everywhere I've been

Breaking Up

Cyclists
damp grass
trees are enemies
Where are all the stars?

So What Is That?

This used to be my bathroom
with my friends
my toothbrush
When I didn't have to pretend
that I wasn't broken by a boy
who buys in experience
a boy who ties my shoes together
then asks me to dance

So what is that?
is stamped on the back of my hand
I try to take it off with soap and water
She says *Yours is darker*
It stands out on the train
A silhouette
Hallucinogenic
I see us setting the table
A supercut of his shadow
I turn the butter knives inwards
this battle is not our fight

The austerity ain't over yet

I catch myself looking
over my shoulder
Am I allowed to call you?
Ask questions about your life?
The line is unavailable

Who makes the rules tonight—

So what is that?
It's something crossed
between holding on
and letting go

This used to be my bathroom

Part One

now the people outside
are friends I don't know

One More Hour

Wasn't the January special?
Wasn't it blissfully
unaware and wonderful
I fell into something
that didn't fall into me
Now I pray it comes back
in more than just sleep
My eyes stick together
just give him one more hour
A phrase used
A white shirt
Sweets in the grocery
Chamomile and honey
Ending the year
in summer
with his words
all over my body

About Me / About Him

There are whispers growing on the wall
He doesn't have to know
how my tears made them grow
He doesn't have to know
that the words came
from under the bedsheets
We should have stayed there
tried to outlast our own body heat
I won't ever let him know
how I took the train to Bounds Green
My face wet because it was time to forget
all that we had ever been
He doesn't have to know—

Hush

have I not just told him
admitted to my sins?

Or does he really think
this is about me and not him?

The Blue Moon

There, there
don't patronise me
I'm sorry that the change in weather
means all I can remember
is who is and isn't here

Frida's flowers are in my hair
I put on *Clair de Lune*
I make plans to visit soon
because what else can I do
I'm bright as one
but love made me feel
like I could be anything
I could be the bright blue moon

There, there
I want to be *there*
The answer was yes and yet
I'm still selling myself as independent
when I can't remember
which door the key opened
And the boy can't spell eternity
Instead it comes out as momentary
He's setting his alarm to leave me
I can't help but want
what no longer wants me

There, there
love is a betrayer
I stand alone in the busy room
to the faceless friends
I want to plea
Someone please adore me!

The only one who doesn't ignore me
plans to court me
one year after two thousand and twenty

But I am not a letter you wait years
before opening

It is there
there
where I see myself again
as the silent but defiant
bright blue moon

I am beaming
for I am one
after I was two

Two

Love Poem #1

He says
Tell me one thing
and then another
but tell me
one thing first

Pillow Talk

I take a pillow
and put it over my head

My skin burns in summer without sunscreen. My
dad used to call me Audrey because I like wearing
high-waisted trousers and keeping my hair short. It
takes exactly nine minutes to drive to school. My train
always leaves from platform nineteen or twenty at
Waterloo. There is something after death. Of this I am
certain. I am perfectly independent. I think Christmas
crackers are overrated. I'm from the suburbs. I love
driving. I bake excellent chocolate chip cookies but I
will burn them in your oven.

I take the pillow off
and you are still watching
Still listening
Eyes asking for more

Thumbs

Winter rests us
beneath her thumb
Our days are rainy and safe
Our nights dreamy and long
The all-seeing-eye comes
when the blood is
rushing to your head
Wet with satisfaction
and then shower water
Shampoo through hair
owls on heads
Lucid memories
and punctured company
Falling asleep mid-sentence
Tugging awake tangled
What could be
at my side
The city outside
continues to breathe
while we play with dreams
refusing to leave

Covent Garden

My parents fell in love at Covent Garden
I've had a drink in the pub
where they had their first date
Every time I pass it
I remember the holiday we took
and taking a picture of them outside it
Click
I'm shopping for vintage overalls
six years later
Click
I'm turning down free tickets
to the musical Matilda
Click
We're buying a scarf because
it gets cold on the border of Canada
Click
I'm stumbling around from too much Tequila
wondering why the Transport Museum
always keeps the lights on
Click
I get my hair cut even shorter
because I believe that nothing
now can ever hurt me

I fall in love at Covent Garden
and believe my parents would be proud

Kissing

Sometimes
I kiss with my eyes open
and I am not ashamed of it
I like gentle intimacy
The slope of his nose
the spots on his cheeks
eyelashes speckled with sleep
I would watch him clean his teeth
or write a grocery list
I am not interested
in the grand gestures
so I kiss with my eyes open
and sometimes
I catch him doing it too

The Spare Pocket

I like to sit through the credits
but will fall asleep at home
in the first five minutes
I am a creature of the night
eyes bright
sipping at the cost of honesty
I like the morning
up and early
dressed and ready
I want comfortable shoes
and sleepy afternoons
Wearing pyjamas
when I'm not in bed
I like watches and rings
washing my hair
writing down things
I count years like minutes
and smell like rose petal jam
I am the spare pocket
for you to warm your hands

Flour

Sweet spots are ankles and
foreheads and necks
Ears and feet and damp hair
Eskimo kisses
interlacing fingers
Eye contact
I only need
to let my lips mark his forehead
fingerprints in flour
We want time to speed up
so we can be together
and then slow down
so it lasts forever

A Weekend

Let mercies on us shower
as hour follows hour
The church bells ring on a Sunday
There are vintage markets with
prints of the world from another age
Would you stay with me
five minutes longer?
Would you be with me another day?

A girl at the weekend
feels like that month in New York
looks like more than just a friend

A boy in winter
smells like the new year
tastes like the future

The Theatre Where I Live

I've heard that I look like the sort of girl
who likes to go to the theatre
What they don't realise
is that I don't go to the theatre
I live inside one
The red bus on Oxford Street
A protest in Trafalgar Square
The French climbing to the top of Piccadilly Circus
at the end of the World Cup
It's all a performance to be enchanted by
But after the curtain closes
it's the spell that happens in the wings of the city
that makes me fall in love
I know all the back routes to the train station
and the streets that wind towards Southbank
I know that there's a pub in Hackney
that leads to a basement with a snare drum and piano
and two dancing strangers who won't be strangers
by the time the sun stirs
It's the honesty behind the performance
and sometimes it ruins the magic
but mostly
it just lets you in
on one more secret

On Writing

I'm sorry I'm up at strange hours
that I'm woken at the calling
that the words find me
no matter how deep I bury under the duvet
You bring home chocolate
with a gentle warning
that the sugar will keep
me up until morning
But darling
the sweet is not the culprit
I am victim to living
and then living again
through pen and paper
Words are not an oddity
you can put away until later
So when I'm up at all hours
scratching into notebooks
tapping into screens
it's a comfort to have the chocolate
that you bring home to me

This Quiet

Last night I drank too much sparkling liquid
It glittered in the lights
and the too predictable music

You gave your head away
as I kept
pouring
pouring
pouring

Oh my love
don't be boring
Let us drink champagne
until the morning rears her ugly head in pain

That beautiful elixir is a liar
I like dancing with you
while my brain is on fire
and everything I hear is
running underwater

I say *I love you*
in a way I don't mean to
but you just smile and
give me your arm to cling to

We're underground
Am I the Eurydice to your Orpheus—
Or is it the other way round?
Is the way my heart sits
outside of my chest honestly that obvious?

There's food in the kitchen
after dark
There's you taking off my boots
leaving an invisible mark

Part Two

It's this quiet I want to live in
Yes
the night is enticing
but with you and tea and marmalade on toast
it really isn't surprising

that just being with you
is my favourite thing to do
and I could go on and on and on
living in quiet for two

Two Stops, Part One

Between Piccadilly
and Waterloo
are two stops
to remind me of you

The Greenhouse

Climb into my garden
and do all the things
spring does to flowers
It is fragrant and floral
(and you taste of salt)
You lift yellow daffodils
and we are transported to a greenhouse
(There's a pulsing in my mouth)
I like to wade through
carnations and violets
to drink white nectar
(it gets bigger)
Plucking petals
while humidity increases
I can no longer see out
(I know something you'll like better)
The glass fractures
(I told you I told you I told you)
The fragrance releases in pillars of salt

Southbank

The lights are strung in ellipses
Propositions hang in the balance
A suggestion to exchange coats
because that's what the liquor told us
Does it make us think in each other's heads?
I like this inside pocket
what do you keep inside it?
There's a clock that might not be there
buildings aren't homes
they are just *there*
The river is still
our hearts are not
Admissions are not confessions
but *I'm Confessin'* is my favourite
trajectory I knew from the beginning
Each light flickers
The imaginary clock strikes
The river awakens
I am that word
You are first
How does it make you feel to hear it?
For me
it's as if I'm wearing your coat
and you are wearing mine
I think I'm a little in love
with Southbank so empty at night

Burmese Chicken Curry

I cook when I'm happy
There is something about
the process of turning
one thing into another
and not knowing how it might come out
My mother taught me
that feeding people dinner
is feeding them love
So I put myself in charge of the kitchen
pots and pans are my friends
The smell of coriander
garlic and onions frying
The spring light outside is dying
I'm learning how to make
my mother's favourite curry
I send a message
Come home now
dinner is ready!
I'm serving the rice
when my phone chimes
I'm ten minutes away
I love you
I can't wait to taste

Love Poem #2

When we kiss
the bones under
the churchyard
all take a breath

Because

Because he hums a three-note melody
when he turns over in his sleep
Goodbyes are stoic
Messages carry little words
Yet he will call
He always calls
He wants to be responsible
for allowing me to save myself
So he leaves the key in the morning
but holds my coat when I run out of hands
He is gentle
I am cared for quietly
I don't like fireworks
I've always found them too loud and obnoxious
Some girls get flowers daily
and that's nice
(for a bit)
though it makes me wonder
are you trying to buy me?
Flowers say they'll last forever
a lie before they bloom and die
I want to walk through things that grow
him in the corner of my eye

The Washing Machine

Like an overloaded shelf
he takes on my mistakes
and plays them off as his own
The wood might break
but he shrugs and says
that this he can take
One finger grazes my rainy day face
Might I make this disappear
by simply breaking my spine
Perhaps the sun is already here
This is what it is
to be mine

Definitions of Love

I see love in kindness
in bedtime kisses
in the one who stays and listens
Love is investing in yourself
It is unconditional
not always traditional
it's following everything through
Love is quiet
when we are intimate
and the crescendo of instruments
when we herald forgiveness
Love is not being afraid to argue
because they'll pack their bags and leave you
I see it in wanderings
far or not
I see it in grief
because mourning means loving what is lost
It's falling without worrying
It's being caught
It's trying to unlearn
what you've always been taught
I see love that is returned and unrequited
Though what is required
to paint love on the ones
who don't see it in themselves?
Love is specific
tailor-made
felt by the rest of the world
in our own individual way

Three

Mint Chocolate Chip

I don't like to remember
the night I walked out of dinner
You spoke in my ear
I still hear it now
crisp and haunting and clear
I don't have a good feeling about this

We were on the couch
one of the countless
nights you couldn't sleep
I had to come out here
I just couldn't breathe

You can have all the mint chocolate chip ice-cream
I'm not afraid of the fever you're burning
I promise you
falling asleep is easy
when you're lying next to safety
So I join you
my body becoming your body becoming our body
and you watch a documentary
and pretend you can't hear me snoring

I would stay awake if you wanted
I would walk you home
I would carry that case on your shoulder

I would leave you alone

Coloured Structure / Birdcage

You're a coloured structure! *No, a birdcage,* he disagrees. He rubs ice down my back to ward off the summer heat. Throwing crumpets out the window. Ordering milkshakes off the menu. Never does my washing up. Leaves an apology in an empty cup. We take turns not sleeping. Worrying about age and health insurance and what is actually worth keeping.

The Unspoken Plea

A collector of coffee cups
painted mugs
wearer of white dresses
but not obsessed
with the idea of marriage
Overground not under
does not hesitate
in wake of grieving hunger
Each day trying to stay put
not to run when tripped by another's foot
Likes to deal in tarot cards
cups and death and many swords
A Virgo not a virgin to unexpected lows
Running late to every date
Hair undone
makeup half done
Arguably pretty
incredibly, unhappily petty
You won't find one in many
with the patience
the stubbornness
the curiosity and pushiness
the unconditional forgiveness
You won't find one in many
You won't find her in any

And I know
you look at every possible anyone
You are just grasping for someone
I'm not the first book you take off the shelf
but I'm still asking you to love me
because I can't seem to do it myself

How We Break Up

Cut me out
a paper person
on display
nothing but time
to hear all the things
you have to say
Goodbye is on the menu
even the moon looks sombre
Now I'm avoiding all things
I used to love to remember
I am a pretender
painting out a background
placing us on it
swearing the happiness
was sustainable
until the plastic ocean got to it
Just lie in the grass
your head in my lap
I am a paper person
this is how we break up

Sense of Self

They hand out silver coins
like I give out love
The air clears my lungs
The clouds gather above
A smile is shared at a table
no alcohol
just ginger and lime iced tea
and eyes that follow me
He just checked you out
she says while we climb
I didn't notice
I was too busy avoiding
the one in my mind
My head is full in the mornings
but I came to this place
for healing
so that is what I'll do
I write letters I'll never send
dance in the garden
sleep when I'm tired
Strawberries and cream
and sitting while
the summer ends with me
I doze in bright orange
I curl into the wall
I still remember everything
I try to forget it all

Part Three

The Honest Truth

Love says
Ready or not
here I come

The Two Bedroom

Why am I trying?
I left number thirteen
Unlucky to some but not to me
I left that two bedroom flat crying

She sways in heels and an orange dress
Her words are the meaning of damage
We both say
He goes back to sex
and I go back to my bed

Why am I trying?
When I could be just as cunning
as you aren't charming
Light me up in red
Pretend you didn't get me into smoking
while I was swimming in your head
I realised only then
that being in love
is as easy as breathing
and as hard as understanding
that each inhale
isn't always paired with an exhale

It was a two bedroom
Inhale
and wait for what comes next

The Lion and the Virgin

He's a lion
a Wednesday baby
a liar
when he says he fears safety
A player of sorts
Mouthful of witty retorts
Continually emptying his bank account
Measuring love
in beats and counts
Bloodshot eyes
from smoke and late nights
He wants to play with fire
because his body is made of water
I get too close
covered in burns
I am the virgin
He eats me limb by limb

Girlfriends are like a Noose

Anecdotes and
phone calls
Popping open the umbrella
(it turns inside out)
Teasing street lamps
littered shadows
and because the washing machine is broken
I soak our underwear in soap
Honeymoon is over
There is possibility
you could have her
But this is starting to become a rope
Wear it around your neck
and wonder

what possibilities lie elsewhere

Part Three

The Tate

The city will give you a taste of sunshine then lock you up for nine hours. The windows spill sun onto the chinaware while you tell a customer she can easily use a tablecloth as a picnic blanket. Everyone wants the things they don't need while I long to be sitting in the park outside the Tate, eating ice-cream, not worrying about what the future decides to be. I dream of swinging on benches decorated with flowers for Valentine's Day. We can be the people we like to make fun of—just for the day. I am strangled by the cusp of the sun, working long hours because London doesn't pay you enough to breathe her polluted air. The night is out. The sun has gone down. I'm not someone that London wants to be around.

The Pendulum

He comes at the fall of day
and as day comes I fall away
We are trying to build a city
out of nothing but our naked selves
and the pendulum keeps swinging
building us up
and knocking us down

A Souvenir

Drink me in
like the green tea
I used to have in the morning
Buy the future
I gave you
then request a refund
when the meaning
of serious
gets too serious
for your loose habits
I am not an omen to be
passed on and on
until there are no longer
hands that haven't caressed my misery
The windows on the
top floor are closing
Recovering is in my destiny
Take a souvenir
and ponder the point of decision making
when the universe without failing
always has her way

Distractions

We have the events
of a century to discuss
so we put on separate headphones
and lie down in the grass

Patti

I drift in loose pages
lost in the breeze
the person they belong to
unable to catch them
Patti Smith might hold my hand
I go back to her book
hoping to find what the relationship took
It is only empty
It is dull
The colour evaporated
from everything I held
I blow my heart out of my lungs
roll around in the acceptance of over
My dresses fit around the body he sculpted
will it still be like that at the end of summer?
We're just kids my friend says
Their eyes are a mirror
Friendship alone tastes sweeter
Squeezes my hand tighter
Offers me more
We're just kids my angel
It was only smoke
the clouds of my breath
on a January morning
I couldn't capture it—
and that should have been my warning
We're just kids
trying to remember who we were
trying to be who we are
We're just kids
you and me
and I go back to Patti

The Bottom of the Ocean

The tide goes out
hush
it wanders around
in deadly pulls
it has a love affair
with the dolphins
with anything that can swim
What's at the bottom of the ocean?
Wildlife changes
as humanity turns through it
Plastic jellyfish bags replace tentacles
It's all so disposable

and what's still at the bottom of the ocean?

For better
or for
worse
you're about to find out

Part Three

The End of June

Three beers and two rounds of Tequila in under five minutes and we're stumbling down the stairs, fumbling over each other. We won this battle, though not the final. I roll on an unmade bed and question if he ever loved me at all. Slurred and frustrated. Beautiful and honest. *How could you ever ask that?* I pass out. It's his turn to watch me sleeping before he throws everything—the alcohol, the feelings, the past six months—up.

The Knife

I cut my finger
while trying to cook you dinner
It didn't hurt
but flesh opened up
and I bled all over the counter

You tried to mop it up
with the sleeve of your jumper
insisting I would be fine

Look
I said
Now you have my heart
on your sleeve
the way I have you on mine

We looked in unison
at the red on grey
a stain pleading with you
to change your mind
to not give love away

The Verdict

The panel of judges
are all masked with his face
I don't know why I'm here
I already know the verdict
The decision has been made

My Way Out

I will slam all the doors if I have to
What else can I do?
I'm not seen
because I didn't go to university
I didn't make amends
I didn't play pretend
I wasn't comfortable in all situations

I am a human
with skin that feels
every brushed-off comment
every attack on my intelligence
every prick of hidden insult
I bleed and bleed and bleed
I am not immune
to distaste and opinions
My qualities do not qualify me
for your precious little pearl
Even though I am the oyster
the elicit opening
to the entire fucking world

On my face
I smile
You and this city smile in a curve that threatens
I say to him
Thank you
for not once coming to my defence
Then I slam the door on my way out

Arguments

There's an argument
at Leicester Square
that took me over a year
to realise was ever even there
If you wait on the escalators
then you can see the three of them
shiny bright from the night
throwing coins in the man's suitcase
If you turn your back
then you see the restaurants
through the entrance
A city cold in February
but not colder than his heart
Start an argument for the sake of it
The concrete eagerly feeds on it
I'd rather dance in the fountain opposite
but I have my own loves that won't commit
So let's all start an argument
for the harm of it
And the buildings quiver
with an orgasm
as we all leave separately
Some on the Northern line
others on foot
I'm heading towards the bridge
for that's where we will talk

Temporary

We're a disposable nation
An obsessive until we're not generation
The scientists say
we have twelve years
or the world isn't going to age
I'm going to combust
from the weight of temporary
from the weight of love under lust

I have one night to stand
so I'm pushed into the arms of one
and then another
(one thing first)
My bones can't withstand
the gentle withdrawal
of the tide from the sand

There's a service charge for love like that
There's a cost on anything and we
with our plastic cards so ordinary
posing as something with meaning
tap them down
emptying a bank account that can never be full
with thinking so thoughtless

I miss your hands
(am I allowed to miss?)
If I tell you this
will you insist my softest moon is amiss
Why do we keep our hearts hidden in our chests?
We should wear them on our sleeves
so when we hold hands
we can feel them beating

The cynics say
There are no longer plenty of fish in the sea
And the scientists?
Well they agree

There's only plastic now
Used and then discarded
and the planet sinks her shoulders

I don't want another bottle to throw away
I don't want to feel the misery between us another day
I want to recycle everything
into words I once wrote for you
then feed this down a line to your distant city
where you just tell me that I used up all your energy

I'll take the plastic now
The turtle has a ring around its neck
it's teaching me how to drown

We're addicts until we're not
We're only looking for one-time thoughts
There is heartbreak in the ocean
and the planet sinks her shoulders

Twelve years
I say
Twelve years until it all just goes away

Four

Loose Cannon

He says he's a loose cannon
and I should have known this
would have known this
had I not been so obsessed
with trying to change him
maim him
tame
his philandering habits

He rides life on a single thread
Daring those who carry scissors
to cut a little closer to his bed
He says
he has to be fluid
It's the only way to hear the music
That's the explanation
the reason I get
the compensation
so he can shoot his fluid
into some girl he's just met

I tell him
Baby
If we're the beach
then you're the water
because there's an entire ocean
underneath your wondrous facade
that I'm starting to discover
I am the sand
Hundreds of tiny, tiny thoughts
making up a crystal shore
And although your tide wanders out
screws around
it always comes back for more

Oh, Baby
While you're fucking her senseless
repeating the same old lines

played out to me in distant melody
consider this
Where do you go when the lights turn on?
When your bender is over
and you're no longer the object of desire?

Do you come back to me?
(the sand and the sea)
Expect my arms wide
open and ready for you
to fall asleep inside
Funny
The bed is cold
I haven't gone out for the night
I've gone home

You can go
and shed yourself of every living past
swearing that each year you step into
might just outlive the last—
Boy
nothing is forever with you
it's 'cause you're too scared
to love something
and then actually see it through
I knew
from the beginning
that we were made to end
So I spent eight months
lying in your bed
eyes closed
living in pretend

When we mend
I'll love you broken
Tomorrow
I'll love you
still

I am a notorious monument

Daughter of Wednesday

in your collection

I am the sand
still waiting for the ocean

Mind the Gap

What if I fall through the gap
between the train and the platform?
What if I fall beneath the red buses
and the gentle kisses he ran from
It is just a city
that is unconsciously lonely
I want a divorce
from the strangers on the pavement
They follow me down to the tube calling out
Let me take you to the London I know!
The London where the cost of a meal
is more than you make in an hour
A roof over your head
can be unheard of until you're dead
Knock on that coffin
and mind the gap where too many have fallen
again and again I lose my grip—

London wins

The Price

Your name is like playing with bees
I want the honey
but it will probably sting

England in Summer

Two are yelling on the street.

I wake first and I'm on top of the bedsheets. You are under them. I didn't think England could get this hot.

I see them through our window beneath the lamp post, obliterated by light, pooled in artificial feelings. I push the window open.

She screams in desperation.

He brings himself to full height.

He could stand on her until she snaps.

"I think he might kill her," I whisper.

"If love hasn't already," you offer. You are sitting beside me, watching. I didn't realise you were awake.

A window opposite opens. The neighbour yells for the lovers to stop. They could be looking at us or them. The boy and girl below walk away in different directions.

It's quiet, this quiet.

"I didn't think England could get this hot," you say.

I look at you. My face is burning. I say, "It's because you're determined to sleep under the covers."

I fall asleep with one eye open, so I can watch you leave in the morning.

Love Poem #3

I hope you're having trouble sleeping
that when you close your eyes
you see every mistake from
the past ten months pass you by

I hope you put on music to drown it out
Your headphones can only
play words from my mouth

Turn on the light
Let it sting your eyes
Remember my question
Understand the intention

The shadow against the wall
is not your own
In her body you came
but couldn't find a home

I hope you're having trouble sleeping
your eyes may close
but your body knows

that you're having trouble sleeping
when I am sound asleep

You're having trouble sleeping
and you can't pin that blame on me

Retrograde

He went back to the night
stumbling in
shadows unseen
I had to fill my mouth with blood
not to ask where he'd been

An Intimate Conversation

Drunken encounters
passion
late night banters
He's topless
lying next to an intimate conversation
he took home for the night
She's beautiful and special and intelligent and
made him feel warm when he went inside
She's also bold
so she asks about his past
The lamp flickers
He frowns
weighing honesty and pain

He says

My past is the face of tomorrow
She is kind and gentle
and has a certain tempo
that changes with constellations
She is naive in the ways of me
but has a history so heavy
that it yields her a philosopher
in matters unseen
She is the moon that pulls my tide
a gravity when I'm lonely
both freedom and somewhere to hide
She slept in my bed
when over one hundred
the thermometer read
and I said she lacked vivacity
and regretted it instantly

She says she'll be forgiving me
again and again and again
because no matter what
she wants me as her best friend

Part Four

Her voice is my constant shadow
her words remind me
of all there is I still don't know
She is the breath you release when you arrive home
the crackling consistency at the end of the phone—

and I left her alone

Understanding splatters over his chest
He looks over

I had the promise of the future
The grass isn't always greener

I don't want to tell the rest

The London Eye Cries

She weeps in a plea for forgiveness
Her wheel turns with tourists who are
taking pictures of the promises
not seeing the hurt she inflicts
I am her neighbour
jumping from borough to borough
as I cup the rejection in two hands
carrying everything I own and everything I don't
in a bag upon my back

My Standard

When you play me
put me to your mouth
my tongue the reed you need to read me
to make music from your dreams
When you play me
what song appears
in shapes and colours
I am more than just
Young
Coltrane
and Shorter
I am the full and beautiful hour
So play me
play me play me play me play me
until I'm coming in your hands
Then watch my temperature drop
the thermometer stop
I'm the dregs of the innocent bystander
played by water pretending to be fire

We're Done

I can hear his heartbeat through the wood
Love is having
the wind knocked out of you
each splinter of the door a cut of before
as he crashes through on his way to what's without

Space tripping
Cloud gazing
My heart
for the taking

He is breaking
more than just a door
It's a cliché
but how painful is it to have to mend a heart
It's like a fractured bone
a collapsed lung
giving yourself to someone
only to hear them say
We're done

I'm not going to hurt you like that!
says the echo of maybe

Yet
I don't know what I would do
with someone who worshipped me

I walk into the night alone
It makes me braver
Lips in liquor
heads in toilets later
vomiting his name before calling him and telling him
that I miss him
Then he is texting
that he can't remember who gave him this number
he lost my name in someone else's bed

Part Four

I'm not going to hurt you like that!
assures whoever comes next

(But I wish you would)

I know I'm still looking at the clouds
when I should be concentrating on what
is now
His silhouette is drifting
and despite everything
despite the constant reassurance of nothing
he is still
the one heartbeat
that I hear through the wood

If Time Had Her Way

In confessions buried
between sheets
our bones we laid
A graveyard to keep
The second hand
stretching too far
My hand
Your hand
I reach
I'm washing the sheets
Mining the dead
The second hand
will always be that to the first
My hand answered his hand
Further on
he stretched his plans
just out of reach

Two Phone Calls

You use self-deprecation
to gain my attention
You already know you're forgiven
for that unforgivable conversation
We're in indefinite miscommunication
'cause you're saving us for future flirtation
Why can you tell everyone but me
that I'm your always sun
I'm where you'll eventually be
You like to hide away that light
I'm telling you now
continue with this
and my shadow will bite

The Meantime, Part One

You ask for time
I ask what happens
in the meantime

The Forgotten Promise

The ceiling opens and instead of the sky
it's just a vortex of forgotten promises
and unintentional lies
They fall like feathers
tickling the back of necks
making their way into every crevice
I'm lonely
I know you know I'm lonely
not to be mistaken as simple insecurity
It keeps me waiting
into lost hours
lost sleep
lost time
Too many tears to weep
I'll reap them
like diamonds for my ears
beautiful until they cut me down
with something I don't want to hear
I'm counting love on my fingertips
leaving hair on your pillows
trying to read ahead in the script
but you keep running off the page
missing dialogue
leaving me alone to improvise on stage
I never said that word
and you won't hear it now
You're the one who kisses in regret
deception is your mouth
I hope you're happy
I hope you hope I hope you're happy
Because I have grass and leftover sun to live on
and that word on my tongue
it ripens with time
The forgotten promise remembered
I won't say it
but that word is all mine

Clarity

Do you think it is something
that comes around every moon cycle?
It is a breath
a chance that becomes
the fog on the bathroom mirror
You wipe it away
convinced that will help you see clearer

Don't Look Back

I don't want to break my broken bones
I don't like this version of myself
I didn't mean to make our love
into something just my own
You looked a lot like me
and in a breath you said
The kitchen is a mess
Pull yourself together
I never said we won't get through this
But what is I love you
when the sentiment is followed
by a door closing
an elevator opening
a taxi coming
round the corner
Don't look back!
'cause you didn't look back at the ticket gates
and I watched another person I let cover me
hurtle towards something I can't create
I could be your new best friend
but I gave that to him
I cut my hair
then again
three times it falls to the ground
There's nothing there
my chest is bare
I've lost the memory of sound
I search for it under my feet
along these south London streets
until I reach Waterloo
where the trains are red and blue
and you
are a navy coat
closing the door
calling the elevator
kissing me over and over—
Don't look back I whisper
or you'll see that I'm not looking either

Five

Daughter of Wednesday

Call me the queen of the weekend
and daughter of Wednesday
Full of woe
I was born to be
what a shame the weekday
failed to see
that there is genuine magic
pouring out of me
In bedrooms
I am royalty

I tease and say I've got the key
he laughs and vows I'm sleeping on the street
before his lungs take hold of me

And we share a mouth
until I get a little too loud
and walls start to build themselves
brick by
brick
The clock face
continues to tick
I stare at it mocking me
while a conversation is held by a river
that must eventually touch the sea

Is there water on my face?
He hands out pennies
while I try and plead my case

I'm sorry
that I feel certainty like blood in my marrow
that I let inner intuition make bold decisions
that I have plans that expand outside of tomorrow
Now
I will be careful with words on my tongue
but not so careful
that we become a lullaby unsung

You can't be scared of something
that could withstand a tsunami
Push and pull
away from me
I'm not as brave as you think
But I will stand in front of you
and drain anything life asks us to drink
And while that's no guarantee
are you not even curious to see
if this love printed behind our eyes
can make it beyond the sea

Slowly
drawn and
tired
drunk on midnight air
he nods
He has much to consider
I nod too
and feel my brain already lighter

They teach us that love gets in the way
I tell him to hand me one of those pennies
for I have one thing left to say

Love
is only a burden
when the one you love
doesn't rise to your horizon
Read it in my eyes
days are how we live our lives
so let us take each one by turn
one
at
a
time
but know a future exists
that could be yours and mine

The clock ticks but the walls come down

Daughter of Wednesday

brick by brick
He reaches out
in our hands we hold the penny together
lapping of waves
beating of clocks
queen of the weekend
there is much to consider

there is much to consider

Otherwise

I thought those words mattered
like I think these words do
but there is nothing I can give
nothing I can say
that will command my grief
that will outwit the grave

I see in hindsight
how I condone my own mistakes
Fighting for something
that would offer me as leverage
I let him have whatever he can take

My nails draw blood
I hold it all so close
I know I met him in a different time
Were we happy in that past life?

People don't belong to people I mouth
when my heart says otherwise

The Cosmos

I'll see you in Amsterdam
I write on the cusp of morning
Sweet orange juice before going away
We'll figure it out
(that's what I always say)
He's lying on his side
fighting indefinite divide
Do you see the cosmos?
Green so green
I don't know where we're at
so we can just talk
without saying anything
until it's the bottom of the glass
and we are the pulp remaining

Raymond Carver

Love isn't enough
but it's a good place to start
He keeps a copy
in his drawer
What We Talk About
When We Talk About Us
I wish I could hold his heart
a little beating stone
I wish I could hold his fear
and tell him that this isn't
science or mathematics
or philosophy or psychology
It's a sound we hear
when the lights go off
when he makes music
and I write about love
I invent the waves on the surface
until I realise
that he will catch all the fish in the ocean
just to give one to me
Choose he says
I point at his chest
I'll have the muscle on the left
He shakes his head and pleads
It isn't enough
I smile and agree
No
But it's a good place to start

Scissors and Glue

The pain is twofold
It blossoms on her shirt
and in her
he sees his reflection
the same knife wound
staining the disaffection
It was not my intention
to take scissors out of the drawer
when you were searching for glue
Know that every time you cried
my bones inside cried too
We share the same corner of fabric
It's red and reminds us of childhood
when kissing was just a game for children
She brushes his hair
He closes her chest
There's something afoot here
feelings we didn't ask for
hearts we have undressed

You Have Nothing to be Sorry for

I'm a broken tap again
and he only has two hands
to hold four years in
Soak up *why*
with skin made of sugar
I think the salt I'm covering him in
will eventually make him bitter
On the contrary
salt makes sugar sweeter
So he lets me cry and I hear his
explanations explaining why
and I ask the hour to hold us in

Some Other Moon

I would draw the shades
of the moon cycle
as shadows on the faces
of the ones so drawn to them

The girl on the window sill
waiting
waiting

Her neighbour up late
waiting
waiting

The boy walking home
who prefers to be alone
except
for his saxophone
waiting
waiting

The one who sits downstairs
worrying their upper lip
fingers trembling over messages
scared their hands might slip

And on the other end of that text
is another who is
waiting
waiting

The elevator opens
closes
The number four he presses

The top floor is bathed in anticipation
He'll knock on which door
My door
they hope in unison

Disappointment is waiting and the saxophone is playing
The girl at the window lifts her hands in exultation
to some other moon she is praying

From her lips she splits him in two
not half
but two uneven slices
because that's what she sees them as
him and her
her and him
puzzle pieces that shouldn't fit together
different colours from different pictures
but shapes that mould into each other
and he knows it too
It's the song he keeps playing
and to the tune
a new language she is creating

The elevator opens
The messages are sent
The key fits the lock
like his body into her's

A smile beckons
he puts the instrument down
The brass is beautiful
even without sound

and the moon shifts
from half to full

Gumption

It was as if you were persuading me to let go
and I was asking you to hold on
Brighter we burn with the gumption to break
We're both just cowards wearing the skin of a lion

You made me feel small
So I picked up that version
of myself
stretched my arms wide to
become the night sky
I am the entire universe
coated in the iris of your eye

and you complained about my energy
then blocked me on everything
Baby
I'm still every grain of sand
but I'm also
the sky in London
the sky you know
like the back of your hand

One day you'll wash up
on the shore to find
I'm not an open door
but in me I've written your name
in case you change your mind

For better or for quiet
Emptiness is heard as much as it's felt
Falling asleep is just a game
of tricking yourself to pass out
Then there's just silence
Hold on
Let go
because this is something
even the universe can't know

Part Five

I'm Going to Keep the Light On

The lampshade casts shadows
She has cried more than him
(or perhaps it only appears that way)
He is recollecting a time when he
took off her clothes in ceremony
I'm going to keep the light on
so I can see your face
They know they must detangle
Neither move
He can see her face now
It brings him no joy
What if he reaches out?

Atlas

He wakes on a Thursday
and more than just his eyes open
It's been two years
(two months two days?)
Two decades
The dream he'd been having
is infinite heartbeats away

Was it a choice he consciously made?

Trying to remember
means sifting through
every regret in his brain
The pain
is what she felt in the beginning
multiplied
by all the times he
could have held her
and instead found emptiness
in someone else

This is not regret
he thinks
This is knowing that
everything lost in the world
is because of me

How to continue with this?
He is Atlas
and the entire woe of humanity
is on his shoulders

Half of Wednesday
there is only one way
Find her
in eyes so green
in everything unseen

Do you remember the
dream he was having?
He saw himself staying
telling her how he felt from the beginning
But she knows that decision
would have weighed more
than the inevitable division

She says

I know you're tired of carrying the world
the world looks a lot like us

It was only two years
Sometimes two decades
Others two minutes

She gives him her shoulder

I'm here now
we can carry it all
together

or we can just let it go

Extra Minutes

London
why are you so busy?
Why are you always in a hurry?
Where is it that you're going?
You can't always be rushing to work or school
or that coffee date you forgot about
until your phone reminded you

Are you faking it?

I did for a bit
Hurrying with the other commuters
pounding the pavements
whirling between tourists
It makes you feel part of the crowd
to be angry at the world
You are slaves to the clock
and I understand
Time is my master too
Just not like you

Because I steal kisses and extra minutes
with my eyes under the covers
I eat meals at the table
and pause at traffic lights
and notice how low
the sun sits in the sky
I like to walk at a reasonable pace to the tube
I don't want to count
the hours until we're through

I take time with goodbye
One more kiss
One more squeeze

I love you I love you I love you

Part Five

Make the most of time
it goes too quickly
Swallow every minute
because sometimes
you wake up and the other side
of the bed is cold

You're in a different room
and you wonder how days
turned to months so soon
London
why are you so busy?
Where is it that you're going?

Is it worth it?

Only time will tell

The Fall

I thought a lot about leaving him
In the way where I am at the window
of a building along the highest skyline
and I think about jumping
only to live through the fall

Part Five

Second Chances

We were waiting for the end
so concentrated on the finite
that we brushed past the prospect
of multiple beginnings

There's Something About the Neighbours

My love
My love

There's something about the neighbours
I just can't put my finger on it

They look upset but I never hear them fighting
Wish I could say the same when they make love
The thing is
I can hear her screaming
and sometimes it sounds like pleasure
and other times desperation

He's a vain one
that boy
he's always got something on that shoulder of his
Takes it everywhere and I think the girl despairs
Is she joking when she threatens
to push him down the stairs?

He likes to stay out all night
while she sits against the door
He finds her corpse in the corridor
still mouthing
We'll be all right, right?
I can tell he wants to reply
but there's trouble sprouting
in the corner of his eye

My love
My love!

There's something about the neighbours!
So I put my finger through the keyhole
and coax the door open

They left the lights on
There is music still playing

Part Five

The table is set with expectations
But the neighbours
are no more

Six

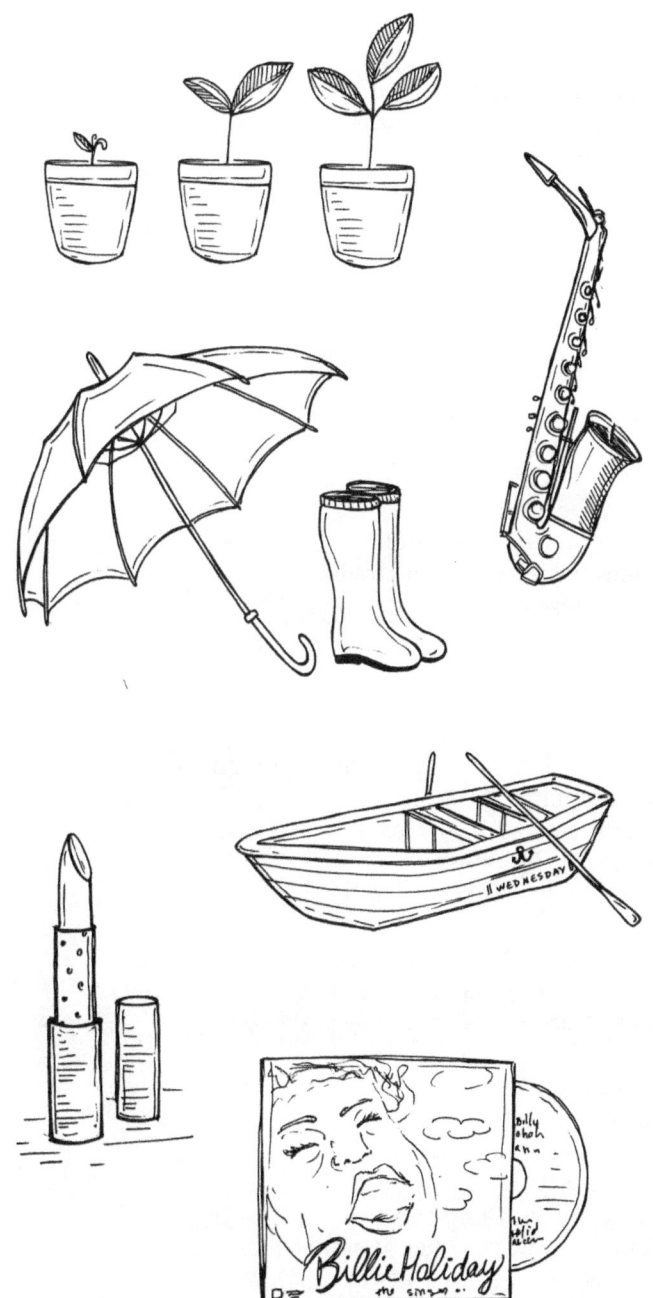

To My Goddaughter

To my Goddaughter
You are about to encounter
the wonders and splinters
this world has to offer

You will learn
that the human heart is a sandpit
Everyone leaves a trace
though some are easier than others
to gently brush away
The ones you cry for
water in the sand
they leave the deepest prints
You must wait for the sand to dry
But I promise you
that no thorn is without a rose

Speaking of flowers
friends are like a garden
Nurture seeds that will grow for you in return
You must put in the effort
to see the colourful rewards
Weed the undesirables
They will only end in a tangle

Your mother is the sigh of quiet content
Your father is the hand to tuck you into bed
You won't always feel as if they understand
the circus inside your head
but they will try
Remember to let them

Bravery is saying
I will be the one to save me
Kindness is being unintentionally selfless
but be selfish when it comes to trusting others
Strength is in independence and dependence
Don't forget to love yourself if you forget everything else

Part Six

You cannot dodge the rain clouds
and umbrellas have a habit of turning inside out
So don't be afraid, my darling
of the water falling
You don't have to dance in it
Just stand and then understand
that there will always be someone waiting
with new clothes and arms to warm you
that is what it is to be loved

There aren't enough words
for what you're about to live
but use these as a beginning
the first chapter
the first song of the album
until you learn to write your own

Slow

I wish I could tell you to slow down
and just absorb
every particle around
Count the clouds
Sit close enough
so you can only breathe
the oxygen from my mouth

Go slowly
I know you have to leave
Everyone has to leave
But go slowly

Plant lips
where you want me to remember them
Repeat my name then your name
make it our name
Undress me
one button at a time
Wash my hair
each strand individually
I promise to smell like home and honey

Isn't it beautiful?
How time slows down when we sit in precious moments
when we don't fear the loss of seconds
the ending of minutes
oh how I live in these hours

If you had slowed down
I would have helped you clean the kitchen and
bathed you in the truth
I fell in love with your ambition
I have never been prouder of you
And although I can't be part of it
you're still my favourite subject
I'll always keep your business card in my wallet

Part Six

I let you go slow
slowly
The way I should have asked you to leave

There is Love

There is love in his eyes as we undress
There is love when he sings my name
as the remedy to his anguish
There is love in his hands
playing like shadows
There is love when he leans
and I'm up on my toes
There is love as we turn
together in sleep
There is love as he takes the fear
I leave within the week
There is love in
genuine questions
Over and over
and if this love is ever over
if I doubt all that was and all that was felt
I will remember his eyes the first time
The words that were his and then mine
I will remember that there is love in us
there is love in it all
There is love that we felt
There is love somewhere else

She Cradled Home

She didn't realise she was home until home was asking her to leave and she was alone again.

In the time when she had a front door, she learnt how to smile and live inside that curve of the lip. *This is what it is to be present.* She covered the floor in Persian rugs and played Billie Holiday on the record player. The walls were painted cream. Furnishings of white and navy and ruby red. Windows she liked to open. An oven where she made banana bread. A key shared until she went to the locksmith and got her own. She was content. She had a home. Cradled in her arms. Loved like a baby. But babies grow in time.

April was terrible. May, a revelation. June, the waves of the ocean. Back and forth. Back and forth. July existed only in the corner of her eye. Then it was time. She rolled up the patterned rugs. Closed the windows. Returned the key. Took a loaf of banana bread out of the oven and left it on the counter. She would save her tears for later.

She said, "Home, you are lovely, but you just aren't ready for me."

The Boat in France

My cousin likes to tell this story
Actually
she likes to tell a lot of stories
but that in itself
is another story
The story she likes to tell
happened in France
I think she was about fifteen
on a boat with a boy with money
(a delusion of charm and dignity)
when he broke that dream and the surface of the water
with a dive of absolute pomposity
While he was underwater
My cousin blinked
and realised that this was her reality
She said
I don't need this
then picked herself up and jumped off the other end
The water became her conspiring friend
pushed her onwards with every stroke
She returned to the hotel
packed her bags and took off on a plane
all the while starting to forget his name

I don't need you
a friend told her boyfriend
I choose you
again and again

I turn to the past in my mind
the image of my cousin
swimming away
my friend telling her boyfriend
why every day she stays
I want to say
Give me a reason
and I might come back

Part Six

I'm not the outline of insecurity
There is nothing to stop me
jumping off a boat in the middle of France
but give me a reason
and after myself
I'll give you another chance

Attic Bedroom

You can't see the stars in London
Not at first glance
But I'm waking up
going to sleep
(isn't it the same thing?)
in an attic with a window straight to you
and closely
(even closer)
you can make out something
(is that a hand?)
A sliver
A white fragment of
burning gas and promise
and hope
I can see the stars in London
There's a constellation with me in them

Love Poem #4

I say
I've seen the night
up close and far away
Two years to see the stars
I set an alarm
beckon me into my widening arms
It's time to know the day

Just a Poem

It's not
just a poem
if it evokes your emotion
if it stirs a place not easily reached

Words are words
are words are words are words and words
with intention
with my blood and breath and flesh behind them
those words can bend a heart
They did mine
and I watched my words bend yours

Poetry
is kindling
for feeling everything
Is that why you claimed the written
as insignificant
as just a poem?

You saw the end
the cruelty of losing a friend
and said
It's just a poem
It's just a poem
It's just a poem—
She's just a poem!

My love, you were wrong
Words are words
and I created words for you
with love and trust and empathy
friendship and integrity
coating them through

I think you're just scared
You were never scared of anything
(only beginnings and endings)

Part Six

of the wreckage
my words will do

It might be just a poem
but this poem
I wrote for you

I Fell Through the Gap

My sin is that I loved him
like I loved this city
Had dreams how it would keep me
wrapping arms of concrete
around my fragile body
There was a tepid warning
steam coming until the kettle reached boiling

Hands make tea
sometimes we leave the tea bag in too long
little patches float on the surface like debris
Drink up, my love
Tea is just smelly water made by me

Hands make London
Hands helping someone with cases get off the tube
Hands when customers give you
chocolate and phone numbers
should you ever be on their side of the world
Hands
when the sun makes an appearance
and we grab our books and sit in a garden
while children run around dodging
the sprinklers but really wishing
the water would catch them

I know I wanted to break up
but I was wondering
if you'd accept me again—
take me back?

London blinks her weary eyes
She takes an x-ray of my heart
understands how I fell through the gap
and it is her turn to apologise

Not Ready

I keep a list of choices
I didn't get to make
Suffocated in a greenhouse
Said goodbye to my father
Said goodbye to my childhood
Half a family but flowers in abundance
I watched as love left the loved
without colour on their cheeks
All the hair on my head fell out
and I left

Say goodbye to your mother
(she's going the same way as your father)

I slept through the new year
But I could still hear
my phone ringing with a possible friend
Meeting made more
I was frightened and not ready
Haven't you been listening?
I looked fear in the eye
and didn't flinch
So unravel me

I'm not ready now but when have I ever been?

Last Year

I spent a lot of time in airports
my hair up
headphones on
Not as much lipstick as last year
I learnt I like rolling into bed
ready for kisses
anticipating each new song

I saw snow for the first time
then again
and again
until I realised it's just icy water playing pretend
like fickle friends
who (by the way) still exist
and I should be open but wary
trust my instincts
farewell the undeserving

Home became a convoluted meaning
Each bed I stayed in
(ten and counting)
reminded me that it's not the place that matters
it's the person on the other side
I cried on the phone
about him for him about loss
Look after my baby
She doesn't deserve the shit
she's been through lately

I'm at the airport again
hair up
and I see them coming to collect me
because they are my family
and wherever I am
England
Australia

Part Six

making other plans
my home is in that familiar face
the gentle hand at my waist
The person I love
who became a place

Permanency

He feared the permanency of remaining
so he went anywhere and everywhere
and settled roots here and over there
then as the green emerged
he grew scared
thrust his hands into the earth
crying about the loss but smiling as he did it
Then it was her face among the flowers
She was whimsical
and quiet but full
of wonder and words
She came into him
and he
after patience
into her
with eyes closed and a low moan
a two-syllabled name
She wasn't what he expected
and that's what brought the rain
Leaving is what they attached to him
Waiting is what they saw in her
Sometimes though
and I would know
it all occurred
exactly in reverse—

Remaining

She feared the permanency of remaining
so she went anywhere and everywhere
and settled roots here and over there
then as the green emerged
she grew scared
thrust her hands into the earth
crying about the loss but smiling as she did it
Then it was his face among the flowers
He was dramatic
but also quiet and stoic
Full of philosophy and lyrics
He came to her
when she feared being alone
Cleared out a drawer of jumpers and socks
so she could have a home
He wasn't what she expected
and that's what brought the rain
Leaving is what they attached to her
Yearning is what they saw in him
Sometimes though
and I would know
it all occurred as it should be
foretold by the eyes of the galaxy

Look at What I Am

I took everything it made me feel
everything in the universe
because that's how it made me feel
I took everything
and turned my skin inside out

It sounds romantic
but remember
that after summer comes the winter
and every smile arrives
with the expectation of tears

I felt like the sky
I felt like the smallest
speck of dust
Still I turned myself inside out
for the wonder of love and lust

I now hold myself
in the palm of my hand
and I understand
that stars burn out
but look at what I am
look at what I am

Look at what I am!
I'm everything it made me feel
I am the light of the moon
the dark in between
I am the quietest corner
I am the beginning of a symphony

Bounds Green

It's an hour on the tube
to Bounds Green
Get on the Northern
then the Piccadilly
it's there that you'll find me

If this is show and tell
then I would show you
a photograph of myself
I'm on a wordless journey
Maggie Rogers in my ears
scribbling down
what I don't understand
crying because people
can see me crying and
still won't offer me a seat
Northern
Piccadilly
Bounds Green
I hope most that I packed a toothbrush
I wonder what you're doing

The telling comes naturally
but not for weeks
I play hide and seek with my diary
Words understand when I'm
too afraid to find them
Until I count to ten
the showing does the telling

Meet me after the Piccadilly line
when I finally return to Bounds Green
It will be less than a week after the party
I return again and again
Holding my hand
I am my best friend

Born from Love

Blink once
and then again
either years come out
or you can see the end
Do you hear that?
Desperation asked into the silence
into collected time so near so far
Hope
it isn't gone
It's exactly where we are
The flowers fall in a shower
There's an attic and a ladder
Petals brush my shoulders
everything gone
returning
There's a misery lost inside of me
I no longer have need
of knowing
Born from love
and rested in it
Blink twice
and I see my beginning

About Her / About Me

She doesn't have to know
that I was the one
whispering through the wall
the saltwater flooded my own heart
as I tried to soften her fall
She doesn't have to know
how I miss the words left on my lips
I asked her what a kaleidoscope was
then threw the covers off
I avoid the Piccadilly line
except for that one night
As I rode the train north I saw her
and she was beautiful still
I won't ever let her know
that I never wanted time to let us go

She doesn't have to know—

and yet she's always at the phone
a fingertip away from care
her forgiveness whispered in my ear

She doesn't have to know
but I think she already does
that I loved her despite what came out
I loved her in the morning

I love her even now

Pluto

There were ribs in that grace period
layered vocals and orgasms
mouthing along as the smallest planet
was deemed no longer a planet

before we had to accept that all this time
it might have just been a comet

It is that acceptance
that I reject
Pluto was small and distant but not insignificant
It is still ninth in line to the sun
You cannot unwrite
what is already done
And because in some ways
we are gone
or the way we once saw us is gone
We can use the bones grown
in the middle of summer
to reconstruct
something else for later
Things are seen differently
but like Pluto
we can't forget what we have been
It's that grace period
and now that I've been on the other end of it
I know why he did what he did
Now he must understand why I climb onto the sofa
let time drift and stay
I'm playing songs I grew up to
asking them to stay around
for me to grow old to
Like Pluto
I won't just fade away

A Second Dedication

He
is the last poem
and I am
the beginning
of the next

So Wonderful!

I think we just made music
that doesn't sound like music
Wayne Shorter in the palm of your hand
What we are passes through us
like an hourglass of sand

On stage is the lonely saxophone
a sign of longevity and hope
We're in New York one winter night
The jazz club is empty
so play for me
and don't worry about what happens
when the sand reaches the bottom
when time turns on the light

Two artists creating
sacrificing themselves for the making
Snow falls in your hair in way of thank you
Don't brush it out
It was meant to be there
I remember it wasn't a sin to love you

You are so wonderful!
We are so wonderful!

Begging you to tell the city
that we've never felt like this before
You're my philosophical soul
a will-o'-the-wisp phenomenon I can't control
I dance as each memory sets me free
the notes are the sum of my body coming back to me
We push the tables together
as if they are the future
But I remade myself overnight
Your words became my words
I wrote those words
and they became my life

It was once a sinking feeling
that the song might be the finale
Now I share the moment with you
It's the punchline about the Titanic
Your smile says you remember it too

You say
Don't forget to take your makeup off
and remember to call your mother
I miss the way you made cups of tea and
the softness of your breathing next to me

I say
I see you in every train station
or when I'm hanging up my laundry
I remember the time we walked home in the rain
books and records under our arms
your voice pronouncing my name

You are so wonderful
but now the sand has reached the bottom
and I should turn the hourglass over
I would like to be on stage under the lights
I would like to start again tonight

It was music that didn't sound like music
They were your words
though now they're mine
The months were so wonderful
I am so wonderful
Forgiveness is wonderful too

I will try to always remember
how wonderful it was
to be in love with you

The Reprise

He says
in the quiet
Do you remember any of it?
Please
anything at all

So I tell him
one thing
and then another
but that I remember everything
every last atom of memory
I remember the beginning
as much as the end
I remember that above it all
he was my dearest friend

At the beginning of August
I sit and watch the clouds
float and change shape

He says
Tell me one thing and then another

I tell him one thing first

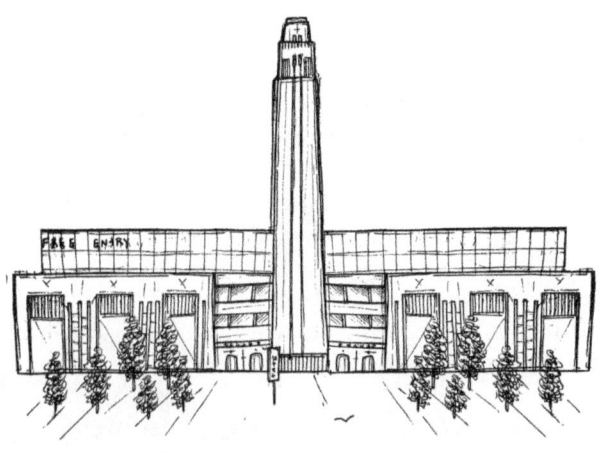

Acknowledgements

There is a homecoming in loss, and I would not be writing these acknowledgements without those who held me through the heartbreak. Thank you; I have made it back to myself.

To Sidney Jean, my editor and friend. Thank you for believing in my words even when I didn't.

To Marta Alvim, you have illustrated my life in a way that makes even the hardest times appear beautiful. I have loved every minute working alongside you.

To Andrew Fraser, for making another wonderful cover. All my favourite stories are ones I've shared with you.

To Allegra Williams, thank you for reading *Daughter of Wednesday* when it was just a document on my computer. I am so grateful for our friendship. To Nafisha Nulwala, your enthusiasm for my books is a blessing. Thank you for helping me spread the word about them.

To those who bought and shared my first book, *Ink for Two*, thank you from the depths of my heart. To Emily Corris, Lena Krakowian, Florence Wood, Miriam Briggs, Amber Russell, Elle Berry and Victoria Mangano. Thank you for your support and friendship.

To my family who I cherish. Especially Katie, Alistair and my favourite niece, Daisy. Also to my cousin, Georgie. To my mum and dad—your love is why I am here today and will be why I am here tomorrow.

And finally to you, dear reader. Thank you for taking these poems and running with them. I hope they help you find your way home.

About the Author

Abbie Amy is a London-based poet who finds solace and understanding in words. It's how she learns to speak. Her debut poetry collection, *Ink for Two,* was published in 2019. Her work also appears online at www.abbieamy.com.

Find her on Instagram @booksbyabbie.

About the Artist

Marta is a scientific illustrator based in London and Lisbon with a passion for intricate illustrations that reveal the hidden details of everyday life. As well as illustrating *Daughter of Wednesday*, Marta has taken on several design and illustration projects under her company House of Illustrology.

Find her on Instagram @houseofillustrology and online at www.houseofillustrology.wixsite.com/design.

www.ingramcontent.com/pod-product-compliance
Lightning Source LLC
Chambersburg PA
CBHW051652040426
42446CB00009B/1092